The Learning Doctor™
shares

FIVE STEPS TO BUILD A BETTER FUTURE FOR YOUR COMMUNITY

What should your community look like in the future?

Lazer Learning Series, Book One

Michael F. Conrad. Ed.D.

Library of Congress Control Number: 2007906632

This edition was produced for Print-on-Demand
distribution by The Learning Doctor™

The Learning Doctor™
2402 Glenshire Lane, Tallahassee, FL 32309

Printed in the United States of America
December, 2007
ISBN 978-1-930301-97-9

WHY READ THIS BOOK?

Planning a strategic direction, be it for individuals or for organizations, uses the same format. This book will provide you with a way to fill in the blanks and create a direction to follow. There are three steps to follow:

1. Where are you now? Are you happy with this?
2. What should your community be like twenty years from now?
3. How do you get there?

BUILDING YOUR FUTURE

The great untapped resource is the power of human energy. One person, by themselves, can raise an issue. But, a unified community of independently thinking citizens, can change of direction and the climate of a county government or a municipality. This guide, and the process of Building A Better Future, is all about accepting responsibility for the direction of your local government. In the United States, we use a dorm of democracy called representative government. We elect officers who make decisions for us. Citizens don't have any authority in these outcomes, but we do have influence, if we provide collective opinions. You not only have the responsibility to Build A Better Future, you care the only ones who can do it. Government, if wise, will listen to the trends and take advantage of your collective energy.

ONE WORD OF WISDOM

Don't wait for government to Build Your Future. Governments are good for implementing directions, but sometimes don't think about what SHOULD be. Being a citizen means more than voting, it means making your vote count by holding yourselves accountable to your vision of what SHOULD be. If you think you can't make a difference, you are correct. If you think that a bunch of you can make a difference, you are correct. The key in any of this is to develop not only a snapshot picture of your community, but to energize people to go beyond government and improve where they live. Only you can do that. The public officials you elected can help you immensely.

Table of Contents

> *"Like an iceberg innocently protruding above the surface of the water, what is visible is community visioning may seem like an easy task. It is anything but easy. Most of what takes place in successful community building is beneath the surface. If you know what you are doing, design your processes well, and have committed people, it will be successful. Don't ever think it is easy. Leaders make it easy for citizens to participate in their own destiny. Community visioning is not about you, it is about all citizens have the opportunity to learn."* The Learning Doctor™

BUILDING YOUR FUTURE TAKES WORK

1. Community Visioning will not solve your problems, but rather identifies them, so that you can set them in order of community preference. This guide book is a way for you to organize, design, deliver, and implement what your community needs twenty years from now. It is the 50,000 foot look at your community. It identifies potential problems, as well as sets directions on future initiatives.

2. Community Visioning is a process to bring citizens together to talk with each other in a non-threatening way. If you want to complain about taxes, the potholes in front of your house that are not fixed, or how inefficient government is, attend a city council meeting. Community visioning is about bringing people together to discuss with each other some of the issues that face you in the future. Community visioning is not about you standing up and giving everyone your opinion about this or that problem. Rather, it is sitting down with your neighbors and discussing the issues that will either help you or hinder you from moving ahead in the future. Community visioning may need to be conducted once per ten years. This is called re-visioning.

3. Like automobiles, there are different types of community visioning, depending on what you want to accomplish, and how much you want to spend. Read the section on types of community-wide visioning initiatives and which one might serve your needs the best.

4. One of the best results of community visioning is revitalizing citizens to become involved in reshaping how their community will look right now. Be it a community-wide celebration of where you live, a cleanup of the parks, a program of arts for the elementary schools, or community-wide education, citizens are the ones who give the spirit to initiatives that make where you live a better place. Too theoretical? Too idealistic? I hope so. This is the citizen involvement that brings life to a dormant community.

5. Involve everyone who wants to participate, but shape the process they will use to get to where they want to be. One reason that community visioning programs fail is due to the fact that the participants hijack the process and turn it into a shouting match or a complaint session. A facilitator will ensure that the process that you choose is followed.

6. Involve the community leaders, the elected officials, and as many associations and churches as you can. If you fail to involve the elected officials, the local Sheriff and Police Chief, you risk having what you propose become irrelevant. The Coordinating Committee will ensure that you have the proper people present, or at least they will have had the opportunity to participate.

7. As hard as you try, you will never get the views and opinions of all citizens, but you can allow everyone to participate.

8. The more you organize behind the scenes and know how to shape the process, the more you will be successful. Shaping the process means you know your meeting objectives and how to organize people to allow them to contribute their opinions without anger or sarcasm. Picture an iceberg in your mind. What sticks out of the water is like the meeting. What you don't see is what is hidden beneath the water. That is the planning part of the community meeting.

9. Not everything you want to achieve is achievable. Be realistic! Most of all, be patient. The key to organizational effectiveness is planning, coordinating, and then trusting all your hard work pay off. Does this always work, guaranteed to work all the time? No guarantees. Recently, a small rural community tried visioning. Outside business entrepreneurs wanted to build a fantastic boat yard, complete with fancy restaurants, condos, and shops. Local residents did not want it polluting their pristine waterways. They tried visioning, but it developed into a shouting match. Be aware that you may need prolonged conflict resolution before visioning can take hold. Too many strong agendas can swamp your good intentions.

10. Don't confuse community visioning with strategic planning. Operational planning looks at what will take place during this calendar year. It is the 500 foot level. Operation planning looks at what needs to be done now. Strategic planning looks at what will take place within the next five years, or in the near future. This is the 5000 foot perspective. Community visioning looks at the big picture of HOW you would like to see your community continue to expand, or what is not being done that SHOULD be done. It gives a 50,000 foot snapshot of the future. These ideas may be used by elected officials, with input from government planners, to shape the future of the community by putting in policies and procedures in place, based on the future as envisioned by citizens.
    Community visioning is a collective view of what the community SHOULD look like. You know what it looks like now. If you don't have a community vision, you remain hostage to outside interests that may not reflect community values.

Summary: Citizens have the opportunity to look down the road to shape how your community will be in the future. Will everything turn out as you envisioned? Of course not. These ideas are just future directions, but with the consensus of citizens. Priorities change, elected officials change office, new needs emerge, but unless you have a vision of the future, you will be stuck in putting out fires of the present, and reliving the struggles of the past. Your children and grandchildren need you to THINK ABOUT THE FUTURE. What you build is what you will live in for the next fifty to seventy-five years.

Will everything you wish for the future come true? Probably not, but more of it will come true if you get a consensus from citizens to move forward on some key issues.

Community visioning is about thinking together, then doing one or two issues that seem important.

FIVE GREAT TREASURES THAT RESULT FROM CONDUCTING A COMMUNITY -WIDE ASSESSMENT OF ISSUES

1. Citizens meet to talk about issues that affect their future.

2. Citizens identify the key issues that will shape the place where they live.

3. People have an opportunity to continue to meet, in order to solve some problems in a way that government can't .

4. Citizens can build community solidarity by involving senior high school students, college students, and faith-based organizations.

5. Citizens have the opportunity to establish a system for community education or adult learning,where issues are freely talked about.

ELECTED OFFICIALS + BUSINESSES + SCHOOLS+ UNIVERSITIES + RESIDENTS +ASSOCIATIONS + FAITH-BASED GROUPS + GOVERNMENT = BUILDING A PICTURE OF THE FUTURE WHERE YOU LIVE

"When all is said and done, what government does best is arouse the incredible power of its citizens to focus on one or two issues, then step back and let them do their magic." The Learning Doctor™

HOW TO USE THIS WORKBOOK EFFECTIVELY.

- This is a workbook to help the Coordinating Committee to organize, design, market, deliver, and implement a vision of the future for your community. Each community is unique.

- Follow each step of the process, but don't think you must use them or fail. These steps are for your consideration so that you won't forget a step in the process. If you choose to avoid a step, ask yourselves what the consequences are of what you recommend.

- Community visioning is all about follow-up, once a plan is made. This plan is independent of any local government, but, like all good citizen-based initiatives, it must include all sectors of the community.

- This community visioning is not a plan for government, although government staff might use it to incorporate part of it into their local comprehensive plan.

- The reason citizen groups fail to do anything, is that there is no plan of action, or what is planned is not meaningful to those attending the sessions.

- Treat this guide as a thought starter, not an activity stopper..

- Making your community a better plan to live is a noble and sustaining goal. It not only helps you, but your children and grandchildren in the future. Citizens are the most important resource that a government has. This is a guide on how to organize people, how they can take ownership of some of the issues affecting their community, and work together for the good of the whole. The negative complainers may never join your community visioning initiatives. Don't let that worry you. Just make sure you include them in the process.

UNCLEAR AND UNCERTAIN

Community Vision	20-50 Years	50,000 Foot Level
Strategic Plan	3-20 Years	5,000 Foot Level
Business Plan	1-3 Years	500 Foot Level
Action Plan by Citizens	Now	5 Foot Level

CLEAR AND CERTAIN

THE COMPREHENSIVE PLANNING PROCESS IN FLORIDA

This is an overview of how your community can grow. Your elected officials are the guardians of this change. You have a voice in the process, if you want to participate.

THE FUTURE OF THIS COMMUNITY
Community tells elected officials what the future SHOULD look like.

Where should we be headed? Revision every 3-5 years.

COMPREHENSIVE PLAN
Elected officials use the information from citizens to update their comprehensive plan.

What are the policies and strategies to run our government? Updated twice per year through amendments.

EVALUATION ANALYSIS & REVIEW (EAR)
Every 7 years, governments must update their comprehensive plan.

What communities need to update every 7 years A review of what worked and what did not? *www.dca.state.fl.us/fdca/dca/EAR*

You should at least know about it. It's the law.

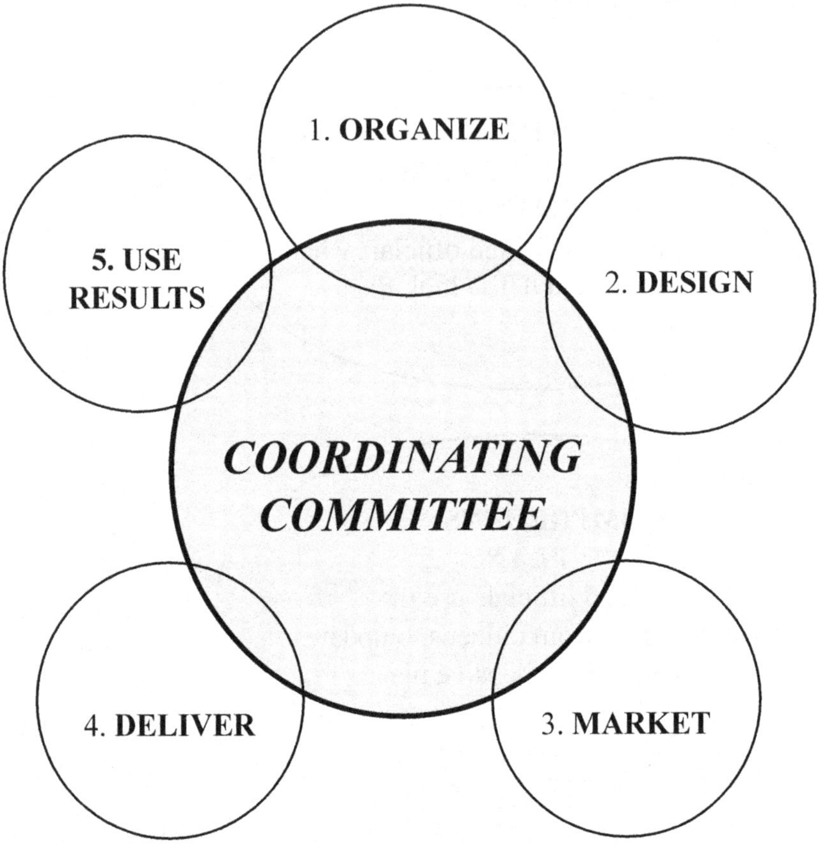

FIVE STEPS IN DESIGNING A COMMUNITY-WIDE VISIONING PROGRAM

WHAT DOES THE COORDINATING COMMITTEE DO?

The Coordinating Committee should be made up of a blue ribbon list of outstanding citizens, those with high visibility. Why? To be perceived as legitimate means the leaders of the community support community visioning. The Coordinating Committee might include at least one county or municipal council member, a champion for citizens' involvement in government, the local Sheriff and Chief of Police, Chamber of Commerce officers, Community College President, homeowners' association presidents, and High School principal.

- The Coordinating Committee selects a person to be program manager, whose responsibilities will be to implement this plan. This person could be a paid employee, or a volunteer. If you have a volunteer program manager, make sure they know your expectations.

- Prevent burnout by organizing into the five functions you see on page 10. Select two members from the Coordinating Committee to chair each of the three subcommittee. Why two chairs? If one is out of town, the other member can take over. Otherwise, you must wait.

- Organizing means you develop a plan of who does what, when, who, and how much.

- There must be one small group that runs the show. Their attitude should be one of making it easy for citizens to get together and talk about issues that concern them. They serve the people by organizing the process. This Coordinating Committee breaks up into three tasks (one, if you are a small community).

- Having a clear ideas of what everyone does makes a very big task easy to do.

ORGANIZE

Select Marketing Team

- √ Promote;
- √ Design Flyers;
- √ Internet Advertise

STEP ONE: ORGANIZE

Select Design Team

- √ Designs Internet Survey;
- √ Designs Categories;
- √ Summarizes Results of Surveys.

Select Delivery Team

- √ Designs Program and Agenda;
- √ Manages Program ..Logistics

Smaller communities may wish to have one team to direct the whole plan.

1. The organizing committee is the heart and mind of the community visioning process. A committed group of 12 local citzens. who want their community to identify what their future should be, is the most compelling reason this effort will succeed.

2. The purpose of a community visioning is to develop a list of strategies of what should happen in your area. This should involve as many people as possible. You won't get everyone, but the goal should be not to exclude anyone from making their comments known, not getting every one at a meeting.

3. Elected officials should be champions of the community visioning but do not need to be directly involved, because of Sunshine Laws. The whole community visioning process is citizen-led and inspired. You will provide elected officials with valuable information on what citizens think should be the future direction of their government. This can be invaluable for governments as they update their comprehensive plan.

4. Involve the media, the school system, the business community, law enforcement, local governments, faith-based organizations, associations, and community colleges.

5. Consider a community workshop having at least three meetings. One to identify the categories of interest and to identify issues. The second to identify what should take place in each of the categories. The third meeting identifies strategies to implement. If you like, celebrate your success with the community by having a Democracy Fair, showcasing your efforts. Have the local High School Civics class sponsor and organize it, then just stay out of the way.

TIPS FOR THE ORGANIZING COMMITTEE

1. How long does visioning take? The answer to that question is, "What do you want to accomplish?" If you want to give citizens the opportunity to meet two or three times, then put their ideas together, it might be two to six months. It depends on who is on your team, how urgent visioning is, and the quality product you want to see come out of the program.

2. There are various levels of community visioning, just like there are cars. The saying in quality management holds up here. Better, faster, and cheaper. You can only do two of them. If you want it done cheaply, you sacrifice quality and time. Put another way, if you want an excellent job, it will take money and time.

3. More expensive is not always better. Determine what you want out of a visioning process. Ask yourself the question, "What are the three or four products we want to take away from this community visioning process?"

4. You can put on a community visioning for as little as $1,000., if you do it yourself. If you hire someone to do it for you, expect to pay anywhere from $10,000. to $25,000. for a basic initiative. Larger communities, county-wide initiatives, and state-wide association can expect to pay over $25,000., depending on the scope of your objectives.

5. If you hire a consultant, make sure they create a customized visioning process for you. Don't settle for a cookie-cutter approach to involving citizens. Slick PowerPoint presentations don't always mean results that meet your expectations.

> TIP:
>
> How do get people to help you organize, design, and implement this community visioning? You ask them.

CHECKLIST FOR ORGANIZING COMMUNITY VISIONING

___ Select the very best people you can get for the organizing committee.

___ Make sure you tell the Organizing Committee recruits that will only commit for six to eight months, then someone else will take over. The Organizing Committee is the booster rocket that gets your community visioning initiative off the ground.

___ Hire a facilitator to be the point person. Don't hire your Uncle George's friend to be a facilitator.

___ Be patient with the process. It works! It may not work, if you don't give it a chance.

___ Small communities may want to have one committee with three functions, rather than three separate subcommittees. Don't forget to bring on more people to help you.

___ Get local teachers to volunteer to be table top facilitators. conduct a little training program for them to let them know what you expect.

___ Don't get into the blame game. Ten people at the workshops is better than none. If you have low attendance, ask yourself what YOU did to get the word out. You may reschedule the meeting for later.

___ More money does not mean better community visioning. Excellent planning ,with the right people to help you, can save money and result in a product you judge worthwhile.

PITFALLS TO AVOID

1. Building Your Future, or community visioning takes anywhere from six months to eighteen months, depending on the level of sophistication you select. Don't rush it.

2. The Organizing Committee is the key to the success of community visioning. If they don't care, don't waste your time and money.

3. Don't think that you can do this by yourself. Hire professionals, or at least get volunteers that have done this before. Don't hire a clown to run your community visioning, unless you want a three ring circus.

4. Avoid stereotyping citizens. Look for help from high school students, community college instructors, and county or municipal workers.

5. Don't exclude anyone from attending any meeting, however, shape how people think, by cutting off long-winded tirades about government that don't fit into your purpose.

6. Solicit Organizing Committee members for a short period of time, such as six months. After that, disband, or reconstitute the Organizing Committee..

7. Thank Organizing Committee members and subcommittees members, if you have them, by hosting a potluck. Bring in the elected officials to show your thanks.

8. Building Your Future is just a way to test how public opinion on various elements. It does not mean that these suggestions will be implemented by the elected officials.

NOTES WORTH REMEMBERING

Write down any thoughts you might have.

TIP:

Citizens' input into where they live and what their future SHOULD look like is critical for urban and rural land use planning.

DESIGN

"It all starts with a plan, only make sure you have a design that facilitates adult learning that does not tell people what to think. Let the community members do as much work as possible. Otherwise, they won't be back."

The Learning Doctor™

What product do you want to have in your hands, as a result of two or three community meetings?

STEP TWO: DESIGN

Logitics

- √ What information do you need to know?
- √ Set goals, resources, place, time.

Design Community Meetings

- √ Meeting One: Categories of Concern plus Action Items;
- √ Meeting Two: Results of Meeting One, plus recommendations for what the community should look like.

Meeting Three: Give Community the Results.

Meet with Facilitator

- √ Review Agenda;
- √ Identify Table Leaders;
- √ Appoint someone to write up the results of each meeting.

TIPS FOR THE DESIGN TEAM

1. If you hire a facilitator to help run the meetings, they can help you design the three meetings. You may wish to have four, instead of three.

2. Have goals and objectives, the three meetings designed BEFORE you market it to the public. If you don't know what you are doing, neither will the community.

3. Keep it simple. If you have three meetings, make them no more than two hours in length. During that time, you should know what information you need to get a picture of what participants think are the important issues of the future.

4. Use this Guide, <u>Building Your Future: How Neighborhoods and Communities Can Identify a Picture of What Their Future Should Look Like</u>. Use this Guide as a template for the three community meetings.

5. If you hire a facilitator, ensure that they are clear about what you expect them to do. Remember. It is your program. Don't give it away to someone else, even if they are a facilitator. They work for you.

6. Find a way to start each meeting with support from an elected official. They can be your champions, and it will allow them to show their support for citizen participation. If you do three or four meetings throughout the county, select commissioners in each of the areas. Although the results of any community visioning are not binding on elected officials, it can give them a way to gauge future directions.

7. If you want to influence ideas for the comprehensive plan, involve elected officials early one.

WHAT DOES A GENERAL AGENDA LOOK LIKE?
(Anticipated length = 120 minutes)

- Register and Sign In
- Purpose of this meeting by Chair of Organizing Committee (5 minutes)
- Introduction of the Elected Official by the Organizing Committee Chair (10 minutes)
- Introductions of Facilitators, Design Committee, Marketing Committee, anyone who made this meeting possible by Chair (5 minutes)
- Objectives for this meeting (5 minutes)
- Short explanation of how to build your future by facilitator (10 minutes)
- Table top exercise to answer the questions: What are the top three to four issues facing this community in the future, that, if we resolved them, would make this a better place to live. (30 minutes)
- Each table reports their top issues. (25 minutes)
- Participants select priorities by placing three dots by their choice of important. Facilitator states results. (20 minutes.)
- Next meeting and why it is important. (10 minutes) Verbal evaluation of the process.

> *"Design a way for people to talk to one another, not just listen to politicians and those with vested interests. Seek consensus, not conformity."*
> The Learning Doctor™

EXAMPLE OF SPECIFIC AGENDA -- DAY ONE
(Anticipated length = 120 minutes)

- Register and Sign In
- Purpose of this meeting by Chair of Organizing Committee (5 minutes)
- Introduction of the Elected Official by the Organizing Committee Chair (10 minutes)
- Introductions of Facilitators, Design Committee, Marketing Committee, anyone who made this meeting possible by Chair (5 minutes)
- Objectives for this meeting (5 minutes)
- Short explanation of how to build your future by facilitator (10 minutes)
- Table top exercise to answer the questions: What are the top three to four issues facing this community in the future, that, if we resolved them, would make this a better place to live. (30 minutes)
- Each table reports their top issues.(25 minutes)
- Participants select priorities by placing three dots by their choice of important. Facilitator states results. 20 minutes.)
- Next meeting and why it is important. (10 minutes)
- Verbal evaluation of the process. (5 minutes)
- Closure

EXAMPLE OF SPECIFIC AGENDA-- DAY TWO
(Anticipated length = 120 minutes)

- Register and Sign In
- Purpose of this meeting by Chair of Organizing Committee (5 minutes)
- Introduction of the Elected Official by the Organizing Committee Chair (10 minutes)
- Introductions of Facilitators, Design Committee, Marketing Committee, anyone who made this meeting possible by Chair (5 minutes)
- Objectives for this meeting (5 minutes)
- Review of the Results of Meeting ONE (10 minutes)
- Table top exercise to answer the questions: Now that we have the top eight categories of concern, what statements do we want to make about each one? (45 minutes)
- Each table reports their top issues. (30 minutes)
- Next meeting and why it is important. (10 minutes)
- Verbal evaluation of the process. (5 minutes)
- Closure

> TIP:
>
> Every meeting has only three parts.
>
> The Opening--remains the same for each meeting
> The Focus--purpose of the meeting
> The Closure -remains the same for each meeting.

EXAMPLE OF SPECIFIC AGENDA--DAY THREE
(Anticipated length = 120 minutes)

- Register and Sign In
- Purpose of this meeting by Chair of Organizing Committee (5 minutes)
- Comments by the Elected Official (10 minutes)
- Introductions of Facilitators, Design Committee, Marketing Committee, anyone who made this meeting possible by Chair (5 minutes)
- Objectives for this meeting (5 minutes)
- Short review of where we are. (10 minutes)
- Table top exercise to answer the questions: (30 minutes)
- Each table reports their top issues.(25 minutes)
- Next meeting and why it is important. (10 minutes)
- Verbal evaluation of the process. (5 minutes)
- Closure

> TIP:
>
> A two hour meeting is about all people can attend, given the schedules people have.
>
> Rural communities may conduct two, three hour meetings, if they think it is appropriate.

A CELEBRATION OF COMMUNITY

Hold the final meeting, a community-wide potluck lunch one month later, on a Saturday from 11:00 a.m. to 1:00 p.m. This gives the Organizing Committee time to present the results of all three days of work. It also allows people to sign up for future projects.

EXAMPLE OF SPECIFIC AGENDA--DAY FOUR
(Anticipated length = 120 minutes)

- Register and Pot Luck Luncheon

- Eight tables on which are the results and maps of eight categories of concern, statements, recommendations, and a chance to sign up for additional projects.

- The Meeting Proper
- Purpose of this meeting by Chair of Organizing Committee (5 minutes)

- Comments by Elected Officials (10 minutes)

- Thanks to all those who participated in the process (5 minutes)

- Objectives for this meeting (5 minutes)

- Short overview of the process. (10 minutes)

- Results of community workshops and what it means to the future. (15 minutes)

- Next Steps (10 minutes)

- Closure

OTHER IMPORTANT MEETING STUFF

1. Don't forget to set up and take down chairs and tables.

2. Set up is usually round tables or two long tables placed together to form a square. No more than twelve at a table (be flexible).

3. Someone should bring ice tea, coffee, water, cookies, veggies and dip, of whatever else you can afford.

4. Print signs up ahead of time, showing directions, arrows, and a big sign outside.

5. Parking may be a problem. Have someone to direct parking, if it is.

6. If you have this at an elementary school, make sure the chairs are big enough to seat adults. Folding chairs are preferred.

7. Bring at least two easels with pads of paper.

8. Write up and print the handouts. Keep handouts to a minimum. Handouts might include the agenda, an overview of the meeting, and anything you want the participants to write out. There is an optional workbook for those who plan to use the three meeting format as outlined in this Guide.

9. Review everything two days before the meeting. Set up the meeting the day before, if possible. Make sure you have extra extension cords, magic markers, masking tape. Check on the First Aid kit. Be prepared.

HOW TO HOLD SUCCESSFUL MEETINGS

1. To ensure that people come back to your meetings, give them a chance to do something or create something that will benefit the community.

2. Word of mouth is the best advertisement.

3. No one wants to listen to your ideas for 30 minutes. Involve the participants in the first fifteen minutes.

4. All workshops should be 80% participants and 20% facilitators and Organizing Committee.

5. Use the agenda to shape how people think. Make it clear at the beginning that this time to work together not a place to vent personal pet peeves.

6. If you have three meetings, you can hold them in three different places, to accommodate participants. Remember that these workshops build on one another.

7. Allow one person to talk, but not dominate others. If you don't, people will not come back a second time.

8. Allow groups of special interests people to participate, but you may wish to split them up at different tables.

9. Don't forget to involve your young people. In ten years, they will be showing you what to do. Set up a community intern program in conjunction with the local High School.

10. People come back to meetings when they sense that some thing is being done to improve where they live. Trust citizens to do the right thing.

PITFALLS TO AVOID

1. Do not design in a vacuum. Do the work in subcommittees or work teams. The Coordinating Committee meetings should be short reports on progress and what help is needed by the subcommittees to get the job done. Again, do the work in small, three to four person subcommittees.

2. Don't do all the work yourself. The more people you involve in the design and marketing phases, the more successful you will be. This is all about enabling the community to help.

3. Design meetings to be 80% participation by those who attend, and 10% talking by you. Too much lecture about your ideas of the future will ensure one thing---people won't be back next time.

4. People don't like to come to meetings. People love to come to groups that allow them to participate in a meaningful activity. Your participants want to get involved. Give them JUST ONE little piece of the pie to do.

5. The more you market, the better your product.

6. Be prepared to get your hands dirty. Nothing happens without work. Community visioning is all about organizing so that one person does not carry the whole ball.

7. Building community means you have to have people present to talk with one another.

8. People want to know that what they are doing is useful to the community. Tell them how it all fits together.

9. Bring in sponsors, such as local banks, the Chamber of Commerce, or churches.

NOTES WORTH REMEMBERING

Write down any ideas you have.

"No one person has all the answers. No political party can solve all the ills of society by themselves. No special interest group controls the will of the people."

The Learning Doctor™

MARKET

> *"It is a waste of time to conduct a community building exercise without a way to let people participate."*
>
> The Learning Doctor™

STEP THREE: MARKET

Collect Your Thoughts

- √ Why do you want to meet? What will you get out of these meetings?
- √ If you are serious, you need a written plan, with a timetable.

One person does one task

- √ Promote in newspaper
- √ Design Flyers
- √ Internet Marketing Advertizing

Speakers' Forum

- √ Two Months Before Event
- √ Week Before Event
- √ Public Schools
- √ Chamber of Commerce

TIPS FOR THE MARKETING TEAM

1. Ask people to serve on your committee for a limited period of time.

2. Have goals and objectives, the three meetings designed BEFORE you market it to the public. If you don't know what you are doing, neither will the community.

3. Use your meeting time to get a general marketing plan, then ask for volunteers to be responsible for one part of it.

4. Select people on this team who know marketing. That way, you won't be starting from ground zero.

5. You can use conference calls instead of trying to get people to meet. It is not always possible, but is a good way to meet, if there is distance involved.

6. Use Internet resources, such as http://www.constantcontact.com., and www.surveymonkey.com for low-cost Email notification of your community. This presupposes you have their Email.

7. Once you set up a system for marketing to the public, all you need do is keep it updated.

8. For those who do not have Internet Email, the local newspaper is always looking for articles of community interest.

9. If you have one, contact the local Redevelopment Agency to help you advertize and offer Email lists. If your community has one of these agencies, you are fortunate.

10. http://www.redevelopment.net/grants.aspx

PITFALLS TO AVOID

1. Don't let one person do all the work. Pace yourselves.

2. Don't forget to enlist the services of local high school or community college students who are studying marketing.

3. Don't be afraid to ask busy people to help you. Busy people who have expertise can do more in fifteen minutes that some one who does not know the contacts.

4. People don't like to come to meetings. Team meetings should always do something. The Organizing Committee looks at how the overall process is going. The Work Team actually makes calls, designs a marketing process, and staffs it.

5. Contact the public more than one time, in multiple ways. You might put something in the paper, then send out Emails to all the Chamber members, with permission.

6. Know your mission. You can't explain to others what you, yourself, do not know.

7. Make appointments to solicit the help of key pastors, business persons, associations, learning institutions, and local law enforcement officials.

8. People want to know that what they are doing is useful to the community. Tell them about the Big Picture.

9. Community visioning that does not build sustainable ways for citizens to participate down the road, will slowly wither from lack of interest. Involve the young to energize the old. Use the old to guide the fresh ideas from the young. Use the young to energize the old once again.

CHECKLIST FOR THE MARKETING TEAM

___ Select the very best people you can get for the marketing committee.

___ Meet for a specific period of time, then disband.

___ People with expertise in marketing will do more, quicker, and cheaper, than someone who knows nothing about marketing but has good intentions.

___ What is your budget for marketing?

___ Can you bring businesses on board and provide them with an opportunity to advertise. A goodie bag for those who attend the workshops is a good idea.

___ Did you involve the high school or community college community? Having someone from the learning community on your marketing team may be wise.

___ How will you advertise in the newspapers, or television. There are always public interest shows that are looking for ways to help.

___ Do you have a written plan on paper, or is what you are doing in your collective heads?

___ If someone on the marketing team get sick, or is out of town, can work continue?

___ Have you thought about grants from Enterprise Florida, or other sources? These grants might help you print up the results for future marketing of economic development.

NOTES WORTH REMEMBERING

Write your ideas in this space.

"Like everything else in life, you can plan the perfect program, but if participants are not ready to learn, you will fail. It is not your fault. Pick yourselves up. This may take two or three attempts before the community is ready to learn together."

The Learning Doctor™

DELIVER

"There are two ways to approach adult learning. You can be instructor-centered, where you know it/they don't, and you want to make sure they do. Then, there is the experiential learning approach that is participant-centered. You may or may not know it/they may or may not know it, but you design learning to explore the collective wisdom. These two approaches are not good vs. bad, but should be used, depending on the purpose of the learning activity. I use both of them within the context of adult learning. If you want people to come back for your workshops, design them so people can participate together and come up with a product."

The Learning Doctor™

STEP FOUR: DELIVER

AGENDA

- √ Train Facilitators for Discussions;
- √ Think of What-If" situations before they happen;
- √ Go through a practice of the agenda before the meeting.

THREE MEETINGS

- √ Divide up the work between Facilitators.
- √ Each Facilitator leads a table-top discussion.
- √ Facilitators all meet before

WHAT DID YOU LEARN?

- √ Build in a way to analyze the training after the first session, so you can correct any deficiencies.
- √ Is this effort worth the time and money?

TIPS FOR THE DELIVERY TEAM

1. The Design Team has made out the agenda, with input from the Organizing Committee and the Facilitator. The Delivery Team must make sure everyone follows the agenda.

2. Each agenda should have stated goals for the workshop at the top of it. See page 21. The words, "goals or objectives" mean the same thing, for our purposes.

3. Goals are what you want to have happen by the end of the meeting. It is good to touch on one or two of them before you launch into the workshop. You can say, "Here is what we want to accomplish today."

4. Try to keep within your time frame. If you are allotted five minutes, don't take twenty. That means you are taking time from someone else. The assumption is, the end time is not negotiated. Don't go over the closing time, no matter what.

5. The Delivery Team should be present at all three community meetings. If that is impossible, get someone to help. If there are no facilitators for the table top discussions, The Delivery Team may opt to be leaders. Let participants do all the talking.

7. Involve high school and college students.

8. Involve local planning officials.

9. If you have an elected official say "a few words," give them a timeframe.

10. See the website: www.businessballs.com

PITFALLS TO AVOID

1. If you have a Bar-B-Que or serve hot dogs, do so BEFORE you meet, not after.

2. Invite college students to be facilitators.

3. Hand out goodie bags from merchants, if you want to go this far.

4. Assign some to register people as they come into the meeting room.

5. Have a sign in sheet for name, Email (optional).

6. Make printed signs telling people to sign up for the Newsletter, if they choose. Their names will not be given to anyone else.

> *"Delivering training is about shaping how people can come together to learn from each other.."*
> The Learning Doctor™

7. Some arrive one hour before to open up and turn on the lights and start the coffee.

8. Hand out an evaluation sheet at the end of each session. This should include:

- How did you like the session? Any suggestions for improvement?
- What did you like most?
- What could be improved upon for the next session.

9. At the last session, ask about what is next. You want to know if people are willing to do something about their future? Ask them to sign up for work teams.

CHECKLIST FOR THE DELIVERY TEAM

___ Meet for a specific period of time, then disband.

___ You are organizing the delivery of three programs. You don't have to be a facilitator, or table top leader.

___ What is your budget for marketing?

___ Introduce the program with a political person. This lends credibility to what is happening.

___ Can you bring businesses on board and provide them with an opportunity to advertize. A goodie bag for those who attend the workshops is a good idea.

___ Did you involve the high school or community college community? Having someone from the learning community on your marketing team may be wise.

___ Do you have one-to-one sponsors?

___ Do you have a written plan on paper, or is what you are doing in your collective heads?

___ If someone on the delivery team get sick, or is out of town, can the program continue? What about a rainy day?

___ Have you thought about grants from Enterprise Florida, or other sources? These grants might help you print up the results for future marketing of economic development.

___ Is there someone to greet people as they enter and sign them up? Get their name, phone (and with permission) their Email.

___ Build a network of citizens for future events.

NOTES WORTH REMEMBERING

Write your ideas in this space.

"Ask participants to sign up for JUST ONE future activity related to this meeting."
The Learning Doctor™

USE RESULTS

"Don't go through the effort of a community-wide visioning, if all you do is produce a piece of paper that no one reads. What will work is that your community looks at some issues and takes responsibility for doing something about them."

The Learning Doctor™

What can you do that government can not do?

√ Don't limit your activities by what government can or can not do for you. Seize the moment.

STEP FIVE: USE IT

Do you have the passion for excellence?

√ Passion means this is your focus in life, at least for the short-term.

"If people take their time to attend meetings, see some possible benefits to their community, and you stop the momentum, you will lose them."
The Learning Doctor™

Organizing for a sustainable future.

√ If your meetings produce no visible change in the community, you have wasted your time together.

What can you do that government can not do?

Don't wait for government to help you in time of emergency. They are too busy putting out fires. Make a plan of action for your neighborhood that details a central place to go for information, for a supply of water and radios, for news of disasters.

Don't wait for government to organize your neighborhood or area. Homeowner associations may wish to devise plans for emergencies, safety, education, travel together, home improvement bartering, and home office consultation.

Community means you care about your neighbor and their well-being.

TIP

Have a celebration picnic of your successful community visioning efforts.

Take the results from this community visioning and identify recommendations for your government. Your group or neighborhood can select those items remaining and see if anyone is interested in moving forward with it. For example, having a mini-park for children.

PITFALLS TO AVOID

1. Go back to the goals you set out to achieve. Results simply ask the question, "How well did we do?"

2. If you don't succeed the first time, try again. Failure is not acceptable. Not reaching your goal is acceptable, if you have a plan to try again. Giving up is not acceptable.

3. People who complain about government or the lack of support are rarely the ones who will fix the problem or deal with an issue. Avoid self-defeating thinking.

4. Economic development that benefits the whole community is a result worth measuring.

5. Seek a balance between a too theoretical approach to change and a practical one. Fixing the moral climate in your neighborhood may take longer than a beautification program. Both are important. Realize that it is possible to have several initiatives going at the same time.

6. Provide opportunity for all ethnic groups to participate in the picture of what their community should look like. Various areas might have their own unique identify.

7. Ask your local land use planner to see the land use map of the county or municipality. It is coded to reflect populations and categories of land use, such as agriculture. Use this map to construct a map of an area you designate. Show on the map what should be the environmental concerns, transportation, health care, education, business, and land uses.

8. Some things government can change, like land use categories. Some things you can change, like lobbying for parts and recreation, a community center, a course on leadership in action at the local High School.

Do you have the passion for excellence?

Give me five people with passion for a cause and I will change the place of where you live. Only five!

People with passion have a clear picture of their future.

Complaining is like having a headache. It hurts you and is symptomatic of something wrong with the whole body.

Move from anger to passion, if you want to change the place where you live.

If you don't have a passion for change in your community, you will always get what you always got.

Your passion should be to continue to make all things new in your community. New ideas, new people to reenergize the process, new ways to do old work, and involving the young.

Citizen created organizations may last longer than appointed ones.

How do you take the momentum you have gained from this community vision of what should be?

A written plan is better than a mental one.

A group of five to nine people having a purpose, the passion to do something where they live, and a determination to be consistent, can have a major impact on their neighborhood.

This is not an easy road. Initially, maybe less than 5 or ten people will support you. If you persevere, more will join. The negative nay-sayers will outnumber the visionaries. They always do. Just remember that criticism without action is just so much bluster.

Organizing for a sustainable future.

SUMMARY OF LEARNING POINTS

1. If you don't do it, your future won't happen as you wish.

2. Government has its limits. The strength of government comes from the consent of the governed. When the governed provide a vision for their community, and it is consistent, fair, and just, there is democracy in action.

3. Leave out the young, at your own peril. Teach the young about democracy by letting them do it with you.

4. Seek to have the principles of your community visioning placed in the local comprehensive plan and land use map.

5. It is easier to improve the place where you live than it is to influence the State or Federal governments.

6. Building community means people of different nationalities, races, genders, religions come together for a common purpose. Just because you never did it that way before does not mean you can't do it again.

7. Special interest issues go further integrated in the con text of community consensus than they do as stand alone ideas.

8. No one gets everything that they want. Everyone should get enough to make their participation worth something.

9. Organize or keep on fighting each other.

SUMMARY OF LEARNING POINTS

10. Democracy works best when you know where you stand, but you also know what you are willing to negotiate.

11. Your community visioning may not work. It does not work for four reasons: the people don't want it, the procedure do not allow participation of all ideas, participants are not respected, and there is the perception that all this work is a waste of time.

12. Build trust in the work groups. Trust those you think are trustworthy.

13. Design three workshops and one community celebration.

14. If you wish to expand this model, you only need to increase the places you hold meetings. If you hold meetings in your county or municipality in one place, you need three workshops and one celebration. if you expand that to the whole county or city, you may need nine meetings and one community celebration. More meetings costs more money.

15. It is best to hire a facilitator/coordinator to run the whole effort. If you do get a volunteer, make sure they have background in designing and facilitating community visioning.

16. There is no magic wand you can wave over a community and force them to communicate with each other. Sometimes community visioning works, sometimes it does not. In either case, move on!

GENERAL RESOURCES

http://www.communityvisioning.com/whatisvisioning This is the website of Oregon's visioning model. Oregon is a leader in visioning and community involvement.

http://www.floridasterling.com Florida has a model for Performance Excellence. This site may be useful to find out what people think about their organization or government.

http://www.quality.nist.gov/ The Malcolm Baldrige Criteria for Performance Excellence is the standard many use to determine how effective an organization might be.

https://www.SCAmes@aol.com Steven Ames is, in my estimation, THE leading expert on community visioning.

United States Department of Agriculture: *www.rurdev.usda.gov/fl*

Citizen Participation *www.hud.gov/offices/cpd/about/conplan/index.cfm*

Environmental Concerns:
www.1000friends.org, www.natureconservancy.or www.natureconservancy.org

NEIGHBORHOOD PLANNING `

This type of planning involves small neighborhoods getting together to identify their needs, plan how to solve them, and implement and working with local governments to form partnership

Neighborhood Planning for Community Revitalization:

www.npcr.org/

Tallahassee/Leon County Neighborhood Planning Process:

www.state.fl.us/citytlh/planning/cmplan/plnprocess/plnprintro.html

Community Toolbox: *www.ezec.gov/toolbox; ww.toolkitparticipation.com/*

COMMUNITY SURVEY _ This site has a community survey model you might helpful in designing your own community survey.

FINAL BROCHURE

gosford.nsw.gov.au/customer/document_gallery/vision-2025. **Don't miss this Internet site. It provides the best example of a community visioning product out there.**

Regional Planning Councils: *www.dca.state.fl.us/fdcp/DCP/partners/regional.htm; www.wfrpc.dst.fl.us*

County Governments: *http//:www.martin.fl.us/GOVT/depts/gnd/sustain/poster1.jpg; www.imaginejackson.org; www.imaginematnatee.org*

Municipal Governments *www.flcities.com/*

Census Information: *www.factfinder.gov/servlet/*

Citizen's Guide to Public Participation: *www.in.gov/idem/guides/publicparticipation/*

Citizen Safety and Awareness: *www.flash.com*

How to Start a Community Organization. *www.hud.gov/organizing/index.*

Design and Marketing: *www.businessballs.com*

TIP

Community participation is nondenominational, nonpolitical, and non ideological.

The focus is on what the community SHOULD look like in the future.

SPIRITUAL DIRECTIONS SERIES

SPIRITUAL APES: Our Journey to Forever, Vol. I..

SPIRITUAL APES: Our Journey From Animality to Spirituality, Vol II.

SPIRITUAL APES: Our Struggle to Be Spiritual, Vol. III.

HOW TO GRIEVE WELL. What Happens to You When You Have Lost Loved One? Spirituality for the Bereaved.

What Happens to You When You Have Lost a Pet?
Spirituality for Pet Owners.

HOW TO DIE WELL. So You Know You Are Going to Die, Now What? A Spiritual Preparation for Life...Forever.

Have You Lost All Your Marbles...or Just Your EX?
Spiritual Perspectives for Divorced Women

Searching for Love in the Garden of Eden. Spirituality for the Lonely of Heart.

If Life is a Journey, Have You Lost the Road Map?
Spiritual Toolkit for Divorced Men.

Spiritual Estate Planning: Can the Rich Get to Heaven?

Is Your Spiritual Life Running on Empty? Overcoming Spiritual Depression.

Resolving Spiritual Conflicts:101 Ways Split-Religion Moms and Dads Can Agree.

101 Ways Moms and Dads Can Be Spiritual Directors: Developmental Spirituality.

Who Does God Think He Is, Anyway? Guidance from the Master.

The Woman Who Changed Time: Spirituality and Time.

Who Rows Your Boat? How You Can Be Happier Than You Can Possibly Imagine.

17 Skills Moms and Dads Must Teach Their Children: Show Your Children How to Get to Heaven.

Who Rows Your Boat? How to Be Happier Than You Can Possibly Imagine.

Three Rules of the Spiritual Universe: How to Choose an Authentic Center That Leads to Heaven.

INNOVATION AND LEARNING SERIES

99 Ways Managers Can Waste Time: Leadership for Obfuscators.

99 Ways Office Managers Can Be Leaders: How to Make Yourself Invaluable to the Organization.

99 Ways Organizations Can Be Spiritual: How to Put Spirituality in Your Organization Without Blowing Up the Place.

99 Ways to Grow Customers: How Does Your Market Grow?

99 Ways to Shape How People Think: Facilitating Processes with People.

JOURNAL OF MEANING SERIES

Come, Share Your Lord's Joy: A Journal to Prepare for Life...Forever.

Spiritual Estate Planning: A Journal to Build Spiritual Wealth You Can Take to Heaven.

You Are My Heritage: Thoughts on How Much You Mean to Me.

The Center of My Life: Thoughst on the Assumptions Underlying What I Believe.

I am a traveler, one who continues to learn who I am, where I am going and how to get there. I need daily centering and God's grace to help me. The Learning Doctor™ is also an organization devoted to providing spiritual resources for adults, such as books, travel, and on-line meditations. The approach is cross-denominational, that is, no one denomination is held up as THE model. The model is our Master.

What have you done with your life? I have had the good fortune to be a counselor, high school teacher, university instructor, Catholic priest, Army Chaplain, adult educator, training manager, a builder of community consensus, office manager, husband, and father, to name a few roles. Isn't that a full life? Am I famous? No! Am I rich? No! I am just a traveler on the journey to... Forever.

What have you done that is significant? Everything in my life is significant. I have not always been aware of how it fits. The most significant thing I have done is to find meaning in ordinary, everyday events, like the smell of the honeysuckle, and the kiss of golden light on the delicate green leaves as they greet the daily, morning sun.

> "Each person is a page in the book of life. What will you write on your page? Perhaps only you will know what it is. Make it a good one, for the sake of your heritage."
>
> The Learning Doctor™

If you could change something about this world, what would it be? First myself! I want to have in my mind the thoughts of Christ Jesus. I want religions to stop killing each other in the name of God, nations to keep from genocide in the name of religion and patriotism, fellow humans to stop killing animals and the land with pollutants, and everyone to focus on the enter of love, and not greed and power. Impossible? Not in the reality where I am destined. Ultimately, I have come to discover that I have power only over myself, and that realization is the beginning of wisdom.

Reflections on Citizenship

One need only take a look around the world to appreciate the democratic foundations of our country. Democracy is not only about one person and one vote, although it is that, but much, much more. Democracy is not about everyone in the world doing government according to the model we use in the United States.

A profound reading of the Preamble to the Constitution of the United States offers the principles upon which a democracy should be based. In this sense, the framers of the Declaration of Independence got it right. They put the correct principles as a foundation of governing. The inherent worth of the individual is raised to a level of inalienable rights, but also protected from coercion by the government or the tyranny of the majority. It is the degree to which we follow these invisible principles of dignity and self-worth that we are a democracy.

Governments' authority comes from the consent of the governed. No matter which political party is in power, they serve the people. With our representative form of government, we elect leaders for a specific amount of time. If the people don't like the approach of those whom they elected, they have the power to replace them.

The highest tribute you can may someone is to call them a citizen. We honor our elected officials because they serve all citizens, to the best of their abilities. Too theoretical? I hope so.

Community building may or may not work, but it must be tried, nonetheless. You have such an unappreciated gift in your democratic way of life. When you shape how your future will be, you tap into that gift and make it real for your family and your grandchildren.

The Learning Doctor™

Made in the USA
Monee, IL
04 November 2026

67382585R00036